Leading high performance teams

Leading
high performance
Teams

A masterclass in team leadership

SEAN CHAPPLE

The terms *Leadershift™*, the *Ice Man*® and *Tent-Time™* are
the intellectual property of Team Development & Training
Limited.

ISBN: 978-1-4457-3170-4

Published by Lulu.com

Book cover design by Rock Paper Scissors
a division of Al Khulifah Group

First Edition

To my mother
for her love and encouragement

Acknowledgements

Thank you to the business adventurers, sponsors and mentors who have supported my journeys and made this book possible.

Likewise, this book owes a major debt to my wife, Sheena and my immediate family for their support and encouragement during my long absences beyond the polar horizon.

Also, for their help with this book Louis Ennis, An Swinen, Keith Tupman, Roy Nixon and Leszek Marcinowicz.

About the author

LEADERSHIP
A TALK BY
POLAR EXPEDITION LEADER
SEAN CHAPPLE
GUEST SPEAKER
GLADYS SNIPE - TEA LADY

Sean Chapple has been a pioneering figure in developing, motivating and leading teams to achieve some of the most remarkable challenges of recent times beyond the Antarctic and Arctic circles. Most notably a return ski to the South Pole, a journey completed by less people than have walked on the moon.

Combining 'on the ice' knowledge of leading teams, with a lifetime of delivering results in senior leadership roles Sean a genuine understanding of the pressures and challenges facing today's leaders.This lifetime of extreme leadership offers tangible and inspiring lessons in high performance, which is invaluable to all business adventurers operating in today's competitive marketplace.

About the Illustrations

The cartoons created by Roy Nixon in this book reflect Sean's polar journeys. Since Roy's first gag, published in 1956, his cartoons have filled the pages of newspapers and magazines throughout the world, with cartoons published in most of the British tabloids as well as numerous publications including The Times, Private Eye, The Spectator and The Oldie. Roy's cartoons have also been an established presence in European journals, magazines and newspapers for a number of years.

For more information visit: ww.roynixoncartoons.com

The Pocket Masterclass

In this pocket masterclass, Sean shares the lessons, experiences and skills he has acquired from a lifetime of leading to provide a definition of leadership, how to lead for high performance and what is needed to be a business adventurer – a high performance leader.

Each chapter includes tips, learning points and anecdotes from Sean's polar adventures to help reinforce key learning with sections to make personal notes. The insights shared in this pocket masterclass offer a useful checklist on your journey to leadership excellence.

Contents

Chapter One

Leadership in
management

*"A polar project is as much about the management
of resources and progress as it is about
leading a team on the ice."*

I would like to spend this first chapter on the subject of leadership versus management. It is one of those subjects frequently debated with different schools of thought on where the differences and similarities are.

The experiences I have gained over twenty years of leading teams in the military, on polar adventures and in the commercial sector place me in the camp that supports the view that you cannot have one without the other.

Authority, Responsibility and Accountability

There are many definitions of management, but put simply, it is the direction, coordination and control of assets. Management consists of three core elements, namely *authority, responsibility* and *accountability*.

Authority involves the right to enforce disciplinary measures or sanctions. A manager may delegate authority, but must retain ultimate responsibility. The manager who delegates responsibility should grant sufficient authority to enable subordinates to fulfil the role while the subordinate remains accountable for actions taken.

The manager will always remain accountable to senior

management, board members and shareholders for the use of delegated responsibility, authority and resources. This includes the duty to act.

Decision-Making, Control and Leadership

If we now look at the roles of managers, we can identify the three essential components of *decision-making*, *control* and *leadership*.

Decision-making in an effective and timely manner is particularly crucial with regard to major decisions that influence organisational strategy. Where possible and in line with the experience, capability and capacity of the more junior managers, minor decision-making should be as far along the line of management as possible.

New managers need to learn very quickly that they cannot do everything themselves. Part of effective decision-making is to let others implement decisions. It would seem obvious that this lesson should be the first learned in business management. Yet surprisingly it is not.

Tough choices are a daily requirement of decision-making. Managers have to hire and fire, to sign off on new strategies, and to risk investments – all of which can lead to stress and guilt. The presence of guilt is not a result of making the wrong choice, but of having the power to choose. That is the human condition: we are a being that chooses. To make a proper decision, and the right choice, managers have to be well informed.

When we consider control, it is in the context of providing continued oversight, direction and coordination of resources - although the detailed activity is often not undertaken directly and is a province of subordinates. However, the reality is that many managers spend more time than they should undertaking control functions.

Managers not only manage resources and budgets, they also have to manage people. In order to do this effectively, leadership is required. Leadership is the art of motivating and directing people into action to accomplish outputs and is a fundamental requirement of any successful manager.

It takes many forms, however it remains one of the least understood and misused skills within the manager's toolbox. Leadership is essentially about interpersonal relations. It is a natural and a learned ability, skill, and a set of personal characteristics that influence people to take desired actions.

It includes the ability to counsel, manage conflict, inspire loyalty, and imbue others with a desire to remain focused on their goals and the task in hand. This emphasis on personal relations occurs in many definitions of leadership. You can read more about leadership styles and leadership attributes in the Resources chapter.

Competence and Influence

To have effective interpersonal skills you need to demonstrate competence (knowing how to do the right thing) and have the ability to influence others.

This can be problematic, because new leaders initially feel the need to prove their technical knowledge and prowess or the foundations of their success as individual performers. Although evidence of technical competence is important to gain respect, it is not what most people look for.

People are more interested in the personality related traits such as enthusiasm, resilience, fairness, humility, confidence and integrity.

New leaders need to demonstrate their influence — the ability to deliver and execute the right thing. Influence through interaction makes people take desired actions. The influence process is where you gain the trust and commitment of others and, without recourse to formal position or authority, moves them to accomplish one or more tasks. Influence over others is also a product of integrity, as well as competency.

By your behaviour, you earn trust and inspire loyalty. This is a vital lesson in an age when scandals and broken trust in corporations, financial institutions and government agencies make daily headlines.

Accepting that leadership is a fundamental part of management is an important step on the path to achieving higher levels of leadership performance.

Summary
Leadership in
management

- Management is about authority, responsibility and accountability.
- The roles of a manager are decision-making, control and leadership.
- Leaders need to demonstrate competence and have the ability to influence others.
- Leadership is about motivating and directing people to accomplish outputs.
- Leadership is about interpersonal relations.

Notes

Chapter Two

Team or Group

"The execution of a polar adventure is usually the easy part, building a team that works together is the biggest challenge."

Before moving into any leadership role it is important to recognise the characteristics, and differences, of teams and groups. The label 'team' is often used interchangeably with 'group' and yet as we understand it, it has a very specific meaning. The difference lies very largely in the direction of action.

A group can exist and yet not achieve much. A team, on the other hand, is action-orientated. It has a clear purpose and it is a purpose shared by its members.

Commitment and Satisfaction

In an effective team, members share a high level of commitment to achieving the common objective and have a high level of satisfaction from being part of and working with the team. Effective teams have members who work well together in an integrated way, with high levels of awareness and appreciation of each other's strengths. This gives them a high capability for solving their own problems. The skills exist and there is a willingness to act.

Of prime importance, from a leader's point of view, is that an effective team is one producing high-quality results. These are the characteristic of an effective team. The qualities of an effective team are, therefore, identifiable, and are quite specific and measurable. Although any group can possess any or all of these characteristics, an effective team must display them all.

The common evidence of a high performance team is that it has a high success rate, it has a leader, but not always the same person, it consists of people who contribute in different but complimentary ways and it operates in a balanced way.

The challenge for a leader is to maximise individual potential and abilities. It is not simply a process of gathering a number of individuals, however skilled, into a group and expecting them to perform as a team, let alone a high performing team.

Tuckman's Model

In 1965, Bruce Tuckman developed his stages of team development model. Updated in 1977 with Mary Ann Jensen, it is still a valued model in today's development of teams and focuses on five stages – *forming, storming, norming, performing* and *mourning*.

Tuckman's model

Norming

At this stage, individuals begin to recognise the merits of working together and fighting subsides. Individuals begin to feel secure in expressing their viewpoints and start to listen to each other.

Storming

The next stage is when all hell breaks loose, factions form, personalities clash and no one concedes. Very little communication occurs since no one is listening and some are still unwilling to talk openly.

Forming

This is when the team first comes together. Everybody is polite, reserved and conflict is seldom voiced. Individuals guard their opinions, particularly the nervous and/or less senior members.

Performing

The culmination, when the team has settled on a system which allows a free and frank exchange of views and a high degree of support by the team for each other and its own decisions.

Mourning

All teams end at some point or change due to personnel leaving or joining. This change of team dynamic will cause disruption. If team members change this may also cause the team to revert to the forming or storming stage.

When putting teams together, or when new team members join, always consider the Tuckman model and manage your team accordingly. By being aware of the stages of your team's development you will know when, and what leadership techniques to apply.

Initially the demands on time can be quite high, and you will find yourself involved in the small detail and in supervising and educating. But over time as a group becomes team moves through the development stages you will able to be less 'hands-on' and take more of a steering and linking role.

Summary
Team or group

- A group can exist, but a team is action-orientated.
- A high performance team has a high success rate, it has a leader, but not always the same person, and consists of people who contribute in a balanced way.
- A leader's priority is to develop and transform the people in the team to achieve an outcome.
- In 1965, Bruce Tuckman developed a model that covered the five stages of a team's development - forming, storming, norming, performing and mourning.

Notes

Chapter 3

The Team Charter

"Agreeing a team charter or conditions of membership is a powerful tool for creating team cohesion and focus."

Having assumed leadership of a new team or group, or on taking over an existing one, your first task is to create a *team charter*. A team charter is a vital tool in your toolbox and creates the foundations upon which to build and sustain high performance. It specifies the purpose of a team, the boundaries of its scope and authority, creates team cohesion and articulates expectations of team membership.

Whoever is creating the team should produce the team charter and share it with the team at its first meeting. This may not always be the formal leader. Individuals should be encouraged to discuss the charter, offer suggestions for changes and agree its final content. Frequently reviewing roles, communications strategies and resource allocation will ensure that the team charter remains current.

It is important that the charter is 'owned' by the team in order for them to become responsible for working as a team within its framework. Team members must be accountable to the team charter. If team members are not working within the team charter framework, discuss the matter with the individual sooner rather than later to avoid damaging team cohesion.

The team charter

Vision
A compelling vision will develop and sustain a culture of high performance.

Communications
Agree how information will be shared among the team, the organisation and stakeholders.

Resources
List the resources needed to accomplish goals (include people and time.

Mission
A mission, the team knows what it has to achieve.

Decision-Making
Agree how decisions will be reached.

Roles
Define each team member's responsibility.

Norms
Define the ground rules that set out the behaviour of team members.

Summary
The team charter

- A team charter is the foundation upon which to build high performance.
- A team charter created by a team will be 'owned' by a team.
- Review a team charter frequently to make sure it remains current.
- Team members must be accountable to the team charter.
- A team charter explains the vision and mission, sets out communication and decision-making processes, defines team member roles, determines what resources are available and sets out the ground rules for behaviours within a team.

Notes

Chapter 4

Leading for Ultimate Performance

*"The ability to know when to lead and when to follow
is a crucial ingredient for developing high
performance team working."*

Business has seen a shift in the popular prevailing models of leadership, and a move away from the top-down management leadership styles of the 1980s and 1990s where apparently charismatic individuals single-handedly shook up and transformed organisations. In fact, recent research has shown that this approach actually damaged long-term organisational performance.

We now see a shift to a more broadly based, participative, team orientated, coaching model of leadership that suits modern times and the make-up of fast changing organisations. Effective leaders are still required to make difficult decisions and take their followers with them, and there are many invaluable insights from the world of polar adventure in this regard.

Leadershifting

Based on my own experiences in extreme situations and often working with geographically dispersed groups and teams, I have developed the concept of *leadershift* - an approach that decentralises leadership enabling freedom of action and initiative.

This approach provides an environment in which the individual with the greater capacity, and/or ability, assumes the formal leadership role. Without abdicating responsibility, it enables a more effective and coordinated use of capacity within the team, engenders a culture of ownership and increases team performance.

It begins with creating a common team language to ensure that team members approach activities in a collective manner, giving them the freedom to act and use their initiative and empowering them to make and take their own decisions.

Working Groups

When I put teams together, I create a number of 'working groups' to focus on key functional areas such as fund raising, logistics and communications. Initially I remain a member of each working group to provide support and guidance as the 'formal' leader.

However, over time I pass the mantle of leadership to individuals in each working group. The speed at which this transition occurs depends entirely on the capacity and skill sets of individual members. The functional responsibilities of each working group also changes depending on the completion stage of a particular task.

Food for Thought

When I set out to complete a groundbreaking return ski to the South Pole the design of our feeding plan was critical. A polar adventurer needs to consume around 5,500 calories daily to be able to ski for 12 hours a day hauling a 120-kilogram sled laden with supplies.

Another important consideration is the weight of the sled. Whatever you take with you, you need to pull in your sled behind you. This includes team stores, spare clothing, communications equipment, fuel and rations.

For rations, the target is to get as many calories in one day and to keep the weight of those items as low as possible. The ideal for one day's ration being 5,500 calories, weighing one kilogram. Initially this involves lots of detailed research. You need to design the composition of a menu considering when the body is receptive to receiving food, and when during the day you actually plan to eat.

Having established the ideal menu the focus then becomes one of procurement, often involving seeking sponsorship from ration suppliers. Once the rations have been procured you then have the time-consuming task of removing all excess packaging, again to reduce weight, and repacking the rations in ready to use packs. As the 'ration task' evolves, leadership responsibility shifts within the working groups.

The use of psychometric profiling tools is a great tool in determining the choice of leader. Some individuals have a natural preference for 'the detail' and are ideal for leading the research stage. Others are more extroverted and are ideally suited to leading the procurement stage.

The final stage of packaging is critical and those with a preference for 'concluding' are best employed here. It is ultimately about identifying those with the capacity and capability to take on role of leader. We will look at how profiles can improve team performance a little later.

Beyond the Office

Leadershift is not limited to 'office' activities. It is equally effective on the front line. When 'on the ice' I leadershift to encourage my teams to take 'ownership' of the journey.

Most polar adventures have an appointed navigator. One person who is responsible for ensuring the team moves forward in the right direction. My approach is to have the responsibility shared by everyone.

During the course of a day's sled hauling, we have regular breaks for a light snack and drinks. When we move off again somebody else takes on the role of navigator with responsibility for moving us closer to our goal.

By leadershifting throughout the journey members gain self-confidence, with trust and team cohesion improve. Having experienced the challenge of leading, individuals are more able to contribute in decision-making more effectively and, more importantly, they begin to take ownership of the journey.

The ability to leadershift also creates the freedom of space to carry out strategic thinking. Where are the strengths, where are the weaknesses, what are the threats and what opportunities can be exploited?

Leadershift requires courage to hand over the reins and it requires trust to allow others to make decisions towards achieving the desired goal. For it to occur intuitively, create an environment that allows this approach to operate following the three rules listed on the next page.

The leadershift rules

1 Provide direction

Provide direction in a manner that ensures the team understands the intentions of the leader, their own purpose and the context of that purpose.

2 Be clear about the output

Tell team members what output they are to achieve and the reason why it needs to be achieved. They should be encouraged to decide for themselves how best to achieve the output.

3 Resource adequately

Allocate sufficient resources for the team to carry out its tasks with minimum control measures so as not to constrain the team member's freedom of action.

Summary
Leading for ultimate performance

- Create an environment in which individuals with the capacity and ability assume leadership roles.
- Decentralising leadership enables freedom of action and initiative.
- Leadershift provides the formal leader with the freedom of space for strategic thinking.
- The rules of leadershift are provide direction, be clear about the output and resource adequately.

Notes

Chapter 5

The

Business Adventurer

The word 'Adventure' is derived from the Latin
adven īre, *to arrive,* and is defined as:
*n. 1. An undertaking or enterprise of a hazardous
nature. 2. A wild and exciting undertaking.*

During my career as an Officer in the elite Royal Marines and as a Polar expedition leader, I have dealt with the harsh realities of leadership and team development in rapidly changing and life-threatening environments on a daily basis.

This challenging career has taken me from high intensity operational conflicts to leading novice explorers across the unforgiving polar wilderness. Environments literally poles apart, yet both sharing familiar challenges in the pursuit of creating high performance in those I have led, and in myself. Over time, the most informative learning has come from journeys through extreme environments.

During high-intensity conflicts and in the Polar Regions, where the unforgiving freezing landscape becomes as menacing as an enemy armed with Kalashnikovs, I have been able to experience and observe how others operate under extremes of pressure and develop strategies for success.

My approach to achieving high performance leadership is borne out of valuable insights into how individuals and teams function, particularly under adversity and at the edge of human endurance. I have not only developed greater awareness of my own capacity for high performance, but also a deeper awareness of how to create and sustain ultimate teamwork and individual performance in others. Over the years, I began to identify that creating high performance teams is not limited to an elite few. Anyone can maximise their team's potential if they apply the right skills and mindset.

There are so many schools of thought on how to do this, many of which focus on external manifestations, such as how to manage a situation or how to act.

Achieving high performance is about transformation. It is about a state of mind. It is about personality and character. It is a combination of attitude, desire, commitment, and much more. It means different things to different people. Leadership is not a science. Leadership is an art.

Learning from Adventure

For decades, adventurers have faced the extremes of uncertainty and risk, where errors in judgement could mean serious injury, or at worst death. Most people's image of an adventure is scaling the highest mountain, battling blizzard storms or sailing the high seas.

While these examples clearly illustrate it at its most extreme, adventure also encapsulates journeys in business such as starting a new enterprise, or leading a project team.

Adventure has particular relevance more so now than ever before. We live in a climate that constantly seeks to mitigate and reduce uncertainty and risk. Unfortunately, both elements are an integral part of business, and how we approach them can have a profound impact on our results.

Ignorance, Arrogance and Complacency

Many teams fail in their quest to reach the Poles despite sharing the same desire to succeed and having similar resources at hand. Most fail not because of the environment or inadequate resources, but because of the wrong mindset in the leaders and team members.

Those who entered the polar wastelands *ignorant* of the challenges ahead, unaware of the hurdles and possible setbacks were doomed from the outset, and for some the price was severe.

There were others who *arrogantly* assumed that they could dust of their skis and adopt the same procedures and processes that had served them well before. They failed to invest the time in developing new team members, learn new things or embrace new methodologies and technologies.

Finally, there were those who became unwisely assuming the good times would continue. They were *complacent*. As we know in adventure and business, sometimes the good times do not always last.

To overcome ignorance on my adventures an intensive period of detailed research takes place. Meteorological data is analysed, accounts from previous adventures are studied and local knowledge sought from those who work in the area.

Avoiding becoming ignorant is also about validation. I take my teams on regular mini adventures to test and evaluate our selection of clothing and equipment. This not only ensures that we have made the right choices, but also to validate our plan and identify possible setbacks.

Investing time and energy into ensuring that teams do not fall into one of these categories is critical to achieving high performance. Not just in the planning, but also during the execution stage. Later we will explore some great techniques, such as the team charter and tent-time, which help leaders and teams avoid becoming arrogant and complacent.

Being a leader is also about unlocking high performance potential in individuals. It is about developing a culture of high performance and, more importantly, maintaining that performance in rapidly changing environments where competition is intense or in times of downturn.

The Nine Essentials

Whether it is putting together a team to make a record-breaking attempt on the South Pole, executing a business strategy, or managing a project, the application of nine essentials will significantly increase levels of leadership performance.

The nine essentials are adopt a positive viewpoint, develop an appetite for risk, venture into unknown territory, expect to encounter setbacks, never give up, trust in self and others, understand the outcome, respect individual differences and enjoy the experience. They form the mnemonic ADVENTURE.

A mnemonic for performance

Adopt a positive viewpoint

Develop an appetite for risk

Venture into unknown territory

Expect to encounter setbacks

Never give up

Trust in self and others

Understand the outcome

Respect individual differences

Enjoy the experience

Summary
The business
adventurer

- Anyone can maximise their potential if they apply the right skills and mindset.
- Leadership is an art.
- Leaders fail due to ignorance, arrogance or complacency.
- ADVENTURE - adopt a positive viewpoint, develop a risk appetite, venture into unknown territory, expect setbacks, never give up, trust in self and others, understand the outcome, respect differences and enjoy the experience.

Notes

Chapter 6

Adopt a Positive
Viewpoint

*"An optimistic leader with a 'can do' mentality will
have a major impact on a team."*

In the current world of global complexities, it is easy to lose heart when things start to go wrong or when unexpected issues threaten to derail even the best laid plans.

An ability to take things in your stride, adopt a problem-solving attitude and stay optimistic can make the difference between ultimate success and failure.

Optimism and a 'can do' mentality will have a major impact on others. While others around you may feel like keeping their heads down, a positive attitude will ensure progress through difficult periods.

Positive Mental Attitude

You may have heard of the psychological term *positive mental attitude*. If not, it is a term that describes a mental phenomenon in which the central idea is that you can increase achievement through optimistic thought processes. It implies that you have a vision of good-natured change and a state of mind that continues to seek, find and execute ways to improve, regardless of the circumstances.

Likewise, to improve, you need to remove any negative thoughts that hold you back. To be successful in leadership, you need to orient on success instead of brooding over failure. The message is the same throughout the book – think positively and it will improve leadership, and team, performance. Find a relentlessly positive leader in any field and one can also find a successful and energetic one.

Using positive language and talking to oneself, releases powerful endorphins, or feel-good chemicals, in your brain. The same type of chemicals released during physical exercise. The connection is that, by getting more sleep, more exercise, and thinking more uplifting thoughts, your energy will soar. A positive mood will raise energy levels, give power to the spoken word, and boost professional presence. Team members will bounce off that and it will make them positive and more productive too.

Successful Failure

During an attempt to ski to the geographical North Pole, a fuel leak from a damaged fuel can in my sledge contaminated the team radio batteries. The fuel caused the battery to short and without power the radio and other vital safety equipment could not be used. This was a major setback and a serious blow to the team who had spent two years preparing for this journey.

Fortunately, I was carrying a small emergency beacon that I activated to alert our home team that something was wrong, although without a radio I could not let them know all the details.

Two days later a light aircraft appeared and, using ground to air radio, I was able to explain our situation. Unfortunately, the aircraft had no spare batteries onboard. It was decision time. With no radio link to our home team do we continue, or do we abort? It would take too long for the aircraft to return with a new battery, as the Arctic sea ice would melt before we reached the Pole causing further risks.

After exploring if any other options were available it became clear - the decision was to abort. This did not sit well with some who, understandably, were focused on reaching the Pole, but as a leader the safety and well-being of the team rested with me and as HRH Prince Phillip said on my return 'discretion is better than disaster'.

Not every act and decision you make will be supported 100 per cent. In fact, there will be times as a leader that you may feel very alone. This is when a leader needs the confidence to make the difficult decisions.

However, landing an aircraft on a frozen Arctic Ocean is not an easy process. Aircrafts need large areas of flat, obstacle-free stable ice. After looking for somewhere safe to land the pilot informed us that the closest safe landing strip was some thirty miles away - behind us. We had no option but to retrace our steps and rendezvous with the aircraft later.

Negativity in some team members began to visibly surface. This can become a real danger in the Arctic where the lack of focus can result in serious accidents. Despite being disappointed at the setback, we had to quickly move on from the setback, refocus our mindset, energy and attention onto the new plan.

By maintaining a positive outlook, I was able to refocus team efforts beyond the setback onto the new plan and ultimately succeed in returning safely.

Positive checklist

Keep learning

Learning develops leadership ability, technical skills and builds confidence. Reading, attending training courses, listening to inspirational speakers and finding a mentor will support the leader's journey.

Keep good company

Socialising with people who are motivated, self-discipline and committed provides drive. People with integrity provide a sense of purpose in your whole outlook.

Avoid negative influences

Nothing will demote a leader faster than people who never produce results, seldom keep their word or always see the negative side of situations.

Summary
Adopt a positive
viewpoint

- A 'can do' mentality
  has a major impact
  on others.
- To improve, remove
  negative thoughts
  that hold you back.
- Thinking positive
  will improve
  performance.
- Remaining positive
  will make others
  positive and more
  productive.
- Not every decision
  will be supported
  100 per cent.
- To remain positive
  keep learning, keep
  good company and
  avoid negative
  influences.

Notes

Chapter 7

Develop an Appetite for Risk

"Challenges are rarely dealt with by sole individuals, so the impact of the leader on the team has to be taken into account."

Risk is a fact of business and life. In business, taking and managing risk is part of what we must do every day to create profits and shareholder value. However, the sudden and cataclysmic corporate meltdowns of recent years suggest that many companies neither manage risk well nor fully understand the risks they are taking.

I am not talking here of gambling the company or taking unsubstantiated risks. There is no such thing as a safe risk. Rather, it is about reviewing the various scenarios and going forward into areas where others are less likely to go.

What is a stupid risk and what is a calculated risk? We can all come up with examples. Taking your entire pay cheque and ploughing it into a business start without a business plan is a dumb risk. Investing your retirement savings in mutual funds in the stock market when you are young is a smart risk. What is risk in business?

When it comes to business, ultimately only individuals can determine that. People and books can only give advice about various directions. When deciding on which paths to follow, we get to the subject of risk appetite.

Clearly, a standout employee, entrepreneur, and a leader all need a healthy appetite for risk and a hearty helping of self-confidence to overcome anything that comes their way.

Moreover, although it is common to mix the two (after all, you need confidence to take risks), do they really go hand in hand? A willingness to take risks is an important part of leadership.

Dealing with Risk

However, it does require judgement and planning in order to minimise the risk of failure. Risk is ultimately about making decisions when an outcome is uncertain and it is for the leader to determine when a risk, or how much risk, is worth taking to achieve a desired outcome. A good leader acts boldly, grasps opportunities and they often appear to have luck on their side.

Dealing with risk is primarily a thought process. Thinking through the risk and assessing the possible outcomes, prepares you for the potential negative outcomes. Considering the early warning signs, you know when assumptions have not been as anticipated. This provides you with the time and space to adjust plans and actions accordingly.

This ability to conduct a test run of any proposed plan is a useful for highlighting potential hurdles, identifying opportunities that may not have been identified before and ultimately help determine if the risk is worth taking.

What If

I always set time aside with my teams to talk through our plan and work together to identify where the potential obstacles are and discuss how to overcome them. This role-playing is a critical evolution before even stepping foot on the ice.

This begins with sessions sat around a map to discuss possible setbacks along our route. These setbacks could include a critical piece of equipment failing, such as a cooker or a serious injury to a key member.

I continually ask 'what if' to try to identify the potential obstacles and setbacks that may occur. By identifying these and discussing solutions a clearer picture of the journey ahead is gleaned and what remedial action I may need to take.

It is impossible to cover every possible eventuality. However, as you encounter obstacles and setbacks by preparing in advance you will move into a problem-solving mode more readily. Some of the thought process may already have been covered and lead to finding a solution more quickly.

Virtual Rehearsals

Another useful technique I always employ prior to my adventures is to virtually rehearsal incident management plans with my support and field teams.

I have my support and field teams sat in different rooms, and using handheld radios, we rehearse a variety of scenarios. I move the incident along in 'virtual time' adding supporting information to help things move along. This is a great technique to identify potential flaws in a plan, clear up any misunderstandings and ensure everyone understands the leader policy.

In the business environment this could include virtual rehearsals ahead of important negotiations or sales pitches, or maybe prior to an important event where the leader can complete a 'virtual walk' though the event.

When conducting rehearsals it is important that everyone who will ultimately be involved in the process participate. Capitalise on existing expertise within a team by having those with most experience lead on discussion points relating to their expertise.

Before beginning a rehearsal, agree on assumptions, this will help to get the ball rolling. Do not forget to regularly summarise and capture findings and suggestions along the way.

Virtual rehearsals provide an opportunity to evaluate, assess and make decisions about the accepted level of risk. Wisdom and judgement on making decisions based around risk improves as experience grows. What is important is the process, which helps to develop risk appetite in a safe environment.

We all have a different appetite for risk, and as experience and exposure to risk increases so will risk appetite.

Risk management

Decide

Those responsible for the task should make decisions. Their judgement, intuition and experience with the task are critical.

Anticipate

Easily control risks by identifying them early in the planning process.

Limit

Accept only risks necessary to achieve goals.

Accept

Risk is related to gain; the greater the potential gain, the greater the risk. To evaluate risk maximise the likelihood of success.

Summary
Develop an appetite
for risk

- A willingness to take risks is important.
- Determine when a risk, or how much risk, is worth taking to achieve an outcome.
- Test runs of a proposed plan are useful for highlighting potential hurdles.
- Continually ask 'what if'.
- Virtual rehearsals help clear up any misunderstandings and agree the risk everyone is prepared to take.
- When managing risks -accept, limit, anticipate and decide.

Notes

Chapter 8

Venture into New Territory

"Getting everyone involved to find the solutions produces better results, and increases team cohesion and the commitment to begin the journey."

The business world is full of examples that demonstrate the value of trying something new. As leaders, each one of us is an entrepreneur at heart, and we love the challenge of trying something new. Leaders of the future need to have the stomach for uncertainty, both among their teams and within themselves.

To be an effective leader you need to have an experimental mind-set. Some decisions will work, and some will not. Some projects will pay off, and some will not.

However, every decision and every project teaches leaders and teams something about how the environment is changing and about how they compare with others.

Self Awareness

Having self-awareness of strengths and weaknesses, or capabilities, is incredibly useful for high performance leadership. Often what a leader may consider are strengths and weaknesses are very different to what others perceive. Continually look at ways to develop areas where capabilities are not so effective, looking at what makes you uncomfortable and stepping outside your comfort zones. Tackling fear and limiting beliefs head on becomes easier the more often it is done.

Starting the Leadership Journey

The first unknown is also learning how to be a good leader. Ask any new manager about the early days of being a boss. Indeed, ask any senior executive to recall how he or she felt as a new manager. If you get an honest answer, you will hear a tale of disorientation and, for some, overwhelming confusion.

The new role did not feel anything like they thought it would. It felt too big for any one person to handle. Also, whatever its scope, it sure did not seem to have anything to do with leadership.

Against all Odds

In early 1995 I set out to complete the first ever ski crossing of Iceland from west to east coasts. It was a journey that many, including the Icelandic mountain rescue service, deemed an impossible journey due to the extreme rugged terrain and unpredictable weather. The journey was also the first time I had managed a 'large scale' adventure.

It took almost two years just to get the project off the ground, initially on convincing others of my ability to manage and lead such an ambitious venture and then obtaining permission from the Icelandic authorities to attempt the crossing.

We succeeded in our venture, completing the crossing of Iceland in forty-seven days. A crossing not yet repeated. The late Diana, The Princess of Wales, sent a personal letter congratulating us on our crossing highlighting courage, preparation, fitness and leadership as key contributors to our success.

Take the First Step

Venturing into the unknown requires courage. The team may want to sit still, not change anything and keep things the same. I talk more about this later, but courage to try something new, despite the crowd, is an inherent skill of leadership. To improve or venture into new territory, a leader often finds that the first challenge is convincing everybody to step out of the plane onto the ice, even if many are afraid to do so.

Having the courage to take the step, venture into the unknown and influence others to follow is a clear sign of high performance leadership.

The leadership journey

Know the team
You cannot win teams over immediately. Start by getting an idea of their capabilities and interests. This can prevent later communication hurdles.

Communicate openly
Teams work best when everyone knows what is going on and who is responsible for what. Nothing destroys a team faster than mistrust or the hiding of information.

Expect the worst
Have team members consider the 'what if' scenarios and they will be more prepared to deal with what comes.

Relax
Leading into the unknown is like the beginning of a polar journey. Everyone is tense and itchy, but when you start to ski everything else but the task is forgotten.

Summary
Venture into
new territory

- Much of leadership has to do with leading people and teams into new ventures.
- A leader may find that the solution is first convincing everybody to step out of the plane onto the ice, even if many are afraid to do so.
- The leadership journey begins with knowing the team, communicating openly, expecting the worst and being able to relax.

Notes

Chapter 9

Expect to Encounter Setbacks

"To maintain forward momentum anticipate the potential setbacks and look at ways to reduce them."

My father taught me to 'plan for the worst, hope for the best, but take what comes'. Only a fool goes into a business issue, an acquisition, a restructuring, and so on, expecting a smooth ride. Business life just is not like that. Having realistic expectations and planning to encounter setbacks means that a leader is far more likely to succeed. This is particularly relevant when dealing with change. People will come up with very good reasons why the status quo should remain.

Resistance should be expected and, rather than taking a top-down authoritarian approach. Recognise that this is something anticipated, and take the time and the effort to communicate and explain the reasons behind the decision, thereby ensuring that barriers are removed, and progress is made.

Confidence and Courage

However, to get over setbacks requires two things: confidence and courage. Confidence is like one of those perfumes that react differently with each individual's body chemistry to produce something unique. The only point on which everyone agrees is that without confidence, nothing happens. Courage is integral to leadership because it is what keeps people moving forward.

Beyond the South Pole

In 2007, I was leading a team on an adventure in Antarctica. We had just skied 1,100 kilometres to the South Pole and our plan was to use giant kites to provide wind traction to pull us back to our start point. It would have been impossible to ski back before the Antarctic winter closed in. Due to the extreme nature of the challenge, seven people had only completed the journey.

Two days into our return kite the wind dropped off and we remained tent-bound for five days. We still had almost 1,000 kilometres to travel and only twenty days before our safety aircraft would leave Antarctica. Our extensive meteorological research had indicated that winds would be favourable at that time of year; however, it was quite a daunting period as we sat huddled inside our small tent in the heart of Antarctica waiting for the wind to come.

As the leader, it was important to remain optimistic, regardless of the occasional doubts that surfaced. This was not a case of burying my head in the snow and ignoring the situation. I had one of the highest-performing teams I had ever worked with. They were all very positive individuals committed to succeeding.

Nevertheless, as the formal leader, and most experienced, I

recognised that my actions, my comments, my behaviour would risk influencing theirs and ultimately risk undermining the project.

Fortunately, the winds did come and we went on to complete our journey in seventy-two days – a journey completed by fewer people than have stood on the moon.

Learning from Failure

However, sometimes setbacks are such that you have no option but to abandon a plan. You cannot achieve success without failure. The two go hand-in-hand.

What is important is not how you deal with failure, but what you learn from it and how that knowledge is used to your advantage. When plans or events do not turn out as planned it is important to take the time to objectively look at why.

To consider what to improve, or do differently, mentally walk through the journey from start to finish, pausing at key moments to understand what happened more clearly. Considering individual own actions, leadership and decision-making also helps highlight any personal areas that need to be developed.

The most important purpose of a review is to piece together the sequence of events and decisions made along the way that contributed to the failure. Often, only a few areas have the most significant impact. When looking back it is also easier to see the warning signs. That is hindsight and it is a valuable learning opportunity.

To capture insights it is always worth capturing them on paper as a list of lessons identified including the positives, as these are equally valuable.

Dealing with setbacks

➤ **Accept**

Accept setbacks when they occur.
Burying your head in the sand only
avoids dealing with the situation.

➤ **Identify**

Setbacks can occur because of an
action or decisions that took place
long before and it often takes time to
clearly identify the cause.

➤ **Explore**

Having clearly identified the cause,
explore ways in which to overcome
the setback with all the team
members to explore all the
opportunities.

➤ **Execute**

Avoid distractions caused by the
setback by remaining focused on the
desired outcome. The goal is to start
moving forward once more.

Summary
Expect to encounter setbacks

- Plan for the worst, hope for the best, but take what comes.
- To overcome setbacks requires confidence and courage.
- Sometimes you have to abandon the plan.
- It is not how you deal with failure; it is what you learn from it.
- When plans do not turn out as planned, explore why.
- Capture insights by making a list of lessons identified; include the equally valuable positives.
- When dealing with setbacks accept, identify, explore and execute.

Notes

Chapter 10

Never Give Up

"In today's competitive environment, by adopting a business adventurer's approach you can push back the frontiers."

An important attribute of the high performance leader is the ability to never give up. This does not mean carrying on regardless with something that is destined to fail, but about recognising that success is achievable, but to achieve it will not always be easy and may take time and effort.

Remember Why

It starts with remembering that a personal choice was made to step into the role of leadership. Remember why you are doing it, and that you are still doing it for the right reasons. By regularly reminding yourself why this particular journey started, you can recommit to it. By reminding yourself of the desired outcome, energy and encouragement can be drawn.

All too often, leaders get so bogged down in the details and minor setbacks that they lose sight of the overall driver that was the original source of their enthusiasm.

I'm not saying be blindly confident or plough on regardless, thinking that by ignoring the setbacks, they'll go away. While it may seem there is much yet to be done, reminding yourself why a particular journey started helps maintain forward momentum.

Personal, team and written commitments are a great source of inspiration for never giving up. A commitment written down and displayed has more impact than one discussed or thought about. The team charter, vision and mission statements I explore later are great tools for maintaining forward momentum.

Keep Walking

On one of my journeys to the geographical North Pole I called the plan *'keep walking scheme of manoeuvre'* and had the catch phrase *'keep walking'* written on charts, printed on mugs and even on the inside of the tent so the first thing we saw as we woke each morning was *'keep walking'*. This helped to create a positive mindset and attitude.

Refocusing Mindset

If you have experienced previous successes think about how that made you feel. If not, imagine yourself, having achieved the result you were aiming for, looking back past all setbacks, realising that you had the confidence and energy to succeed.

When you have negative thoughts, which are natural and normal, it is good to catch them and acknowledge them. When they surface, say it, express it and exorcise it. Later I will share a technique with you called *tent-time* which is a great way to deal with negative thoughts.

Sometimes you may see a situation differently to what is seen by team members. By engaging with team members and encouraging everyone to think about the situation will help you avoid becoming isolated in the thought process. However, what is important is that other team members think about the situation independently and not collectively.

All the facts and information available should be gathered for you to weigh it all up before making a decision. Occasionally taking a step back to review decisions made and to celebrate achievements is a useful technique. It is too easy to lose focus and momentum because of fears that the progress that you want to make is not happening.

Maintain Momentum

During a journey to the magnetic North Pole one of my team members sustained frostbite and I made the decision to have him airlifted off the ice. This had a demoralising effect on the remainder of the team. We had lost a valued team member, and our goal to complete the journey 'unsupported' had now changed.

With the loss of a team member we were now classed in the adventure community as being 'supported' with our extracted team member being considered a 'porter' who had supported part of the journey.

My priority was to realign focus back on the journey, and a new goal 'to reach the pole'. As soon as the emergency airlift had been completed I briefed the team that we would immediately continue and we completed a four hour ski before setting up camp. We could have waited until the following day before carrying on, but it was important for me to have everyone's attention on the 'here and now' as quickly as possible.

Strong leadership often means stopping what you are doing; taking a physical step back from the situation and thinking through the reality of where you are right now and what you are doing. Do not judge whether what is being done is good or bad, or if the team is as far forward as it ought to be.

Never give up

Recall
Recall what has worked before
and make alterations for the
current circumstances.

Commit
Commit, remain forward
focused and remain confident
of success.

Think
Avoid group think. Encourage
independent focused thinking.

Step Back
Occasionally take a step back
to review decisions made.

Perspective
Keep everything in perspective.

Summary
Never give up

- Remind yourself of the outcome to draw encouragement.
- Personal and team commitments are a source of inspiration.
- When you have a negative or destructive thought, say it, express it and exorcise it.
- Occasionally step back to review decisions and celebrate achievements.
- Do not judge whether what you are doing is good or bad, do not judge if you are as far forward as you ought to be.
- Recall, commit, think, step back and keep everything in perspective.

Notes

Chapter 11

Trust in Yourself and Others

*"I always encourage my fellow team members to take
ownership and responsibility for the journey."*

I have noticed a significant difference between the levels of self-trust in the world of exploration and in the world of business. In the world of adventure, leaders have a strong and unshakeable belief in their ability to complete a challenging assignment. It is not arrogance, but a quiet self-confidence. In my work with senior business managers and leaders, I have been surprised just how many find it difficult to trust themselves and their ability to deliver.

Take Positive Action

Encouraging people to trust you requires positive action. It is not something an organisation can mandate a person to do. Commit yourself to being trustworthy and make sure your actions reflect this. Teams never reach true high performance if senior leadership does not create a climate that demonstrates its complete faith in them.

This does not mean abdicating responsibility for their results. It simply means letting team members get on with dealing with their issues; people own what they help to create. At lower levels, the priority is to keep everyone focused on immediate tasks and getting the work done.

At higher leadership levels, the driver approach does not work anymore. Decision styles become more about listening than telling, more about understanding than directing and exchange the hard-edged decisive and hierarchic modes of leadership in favour of the more inclusive flexible and integrative styles.

Personal Character

You may have been surprised in the past by how difficult it is to earn people's respect and trust. Maybe you were shocked, and even insulted, that your expertise and record of accomplishment did not speak for themselves. To fix this dilemma you need to demonstrate your character - the intention to do the right thing. This is of particular importance to subordinates, who tend to analyse every statement and non-verbal gesture for signs of the new leader's motives.

Trust is difficult to describe or define. We know when it is there and when it is not. We trust people who are predictable – not in the dull, plodding sense – but because we will receive a consistent response. Trust provides the motivation and energy that makes it possible for high performance team to work.

Empowerment

Another way to generate trust is to empower team members. This means letting a member of a team carry out a responsibility that would normally fall to you. It involves specifying what results are to be achieved, with what resources, and within what limits of authority. It leaves the individual free to choose how to achieve results.

To empower you must have the courage to take the risks involved, remain accountable for any mistakes, have the patience to wait for results and always have trust and faith in your team. In my experience, empowerment significantly improves performance by making better use of individual and team capabilities. It provides greater discretion in decision-making, thus enriching tasks and increasing satisfaction.

Better information is often available nearer the point of action with decisions taken sooner. This increases the output of the team. Empowerment aids in gaining commitment through involvement in decisions, improves motivation and increases the willingness to work extra when the pressure is on. This makes the teams work more satisfactorily and gains team engagement.

Team members develop by increasing their knowledge, skills and versatility that in turn will make their contribution to the team effort more powerful. This improves each member's competence. Finally, it saves time for more productive tasks. Empowerment needs to be a conscious and thought-through process.

Hidden Dangers

One of the greatest dangers encountered in Antarctica are the crevasse fields. A crevasse is a crack in an ice sheet – in Antarctica the ice sheet, which covers the continent, is up to 4 miles thick – they often have vertical or near-vertical walls and are often covered, but not necessarily filled, by a snow bridge made of the previous year's snow. These cracks often appear in large numbers over several miles long. Falling into a hidden crevasse covered by a weak snow bridge is a real risk.

All my teams complete training in crevasse rescue techniques should someone fall into a crevasse, but the real skill is the ability to cross a snow bridge safely and this takes practice.

To lead a team across every crevasse snow bridge would be mentally and physically demanding for me, and unsustainable on a long polar journey.

Therefore, I always encourage team members to take the lead in crossing snow bridges to build upon their experiences and develop self-confidence and mutual trust within the team. Initially under my close supervision, as their confidence builds I can empower them to keep us moving safely forwards towards our goal and focus my efforts on other areas.

Problems can occur with empowerment if you become insular and isolated in your decision-making and control of information. You have to learn to release control, make fewer checks and allow the team freedom to take action.

If you are afraid of the loss of control, or not naturally inclined to take risks, spend more time on planning to minimise the risks involved. The rationale that it is quicker and easier to do it yourself may produce immediate results, but for long-term high-performance, you must trust the team to do a good job. This requires investing time and effort to explain what you want achieved and provide guidance when needed.

Generating trust

✓ **Be consistent**

Be consistent in what you do as a leader. Carry out your own task effectively both internally and to the wider environment.

✓ **Be committed**

Demonstrate commitment through repeated observable actions.

✓ **Be compassionate**

Empathise with teams by understanding how they feel and view the world.

Summary
Trust in yourself and others

- Encouraging trust requires positive action.
- People own what they help to create.
- Empowerment gains commitment through involvement.
- Problems can occur when leaders become insular and keep decision-making and information to themselves.
- The rationale that it is quicker and easier to do it yourself will only produce short-term results.
- To generate trust be consistent, be committed and be compassionate.

Notes

Chapter 12

Understand the Outcome

"The most valued lesson I have learnt from polar travel is start out with the end in mind."

One thing that I have learnt over the years is the value of starting out with the end in mind. Whatever the project or challenge, spending time on understanding and getting agreement on 'what success looks like' pays enormous dividends because it increases the chances of achieving that success considerably.

In today's fast-paced environment and the reliance on information technology, the leader has to deal with the variety of administrative responsibilities once delegated to junior staff. This will draw heavily on time and resources if not managed, organised and dealt with effectively.

Research

Researching as much information as quickly as possible helps you understand the potential of what you will be dealing with. Those who have already dealt with similar situations can provide a wealth of experience.

Get Organised and Plan

To organise effectively requires systems or processes to be out in place. These should not stifle the initiative or freedom of action of a team, but provide an orderly and structured way of doing business. This will provide a framework to support a team moving closer towards goals. Organisation is the best way for a leader to understand the outcome. The last thing a leader wants to worry about is a lack of planning. Enough other unknown variables demand attention.

You may have heard the old saying 'If you fail to plan, you are planning to fail.' If not, then it is very good advice, as planning is essential for a number of reasons.

To plan you first need a plan of approach. It is important to know what resources are available, what they are capable of and what is not available. The methodology for tackling the new problem or issue can then be designed as best as possible your. Following a plan will keep everyone on track when unpredictability strikes.

The biggest risk of the unknown is not being ready for an unpredictable factor. Flexibility allows for the adjustment midstream to the new factor and keeps progress moving forward.

Planning is about applying resources (people, finances, time and material) to the mental road leading to goals and objectives. Time should be spent to really focus on what shape the desired outcome will take. Without this how can you plan your journey to achieve it?

Through planning, you retain more control of events as they unfold and you do not find yourself reacting as issues occur, or fire fighting when they escalate because you lacked the time and resources to deal with them before they became major problems.

Through planning you can more effectively allocate your resources to achieve more productive results and allow themselves the freedom of space to monitor progress and respond in a more timely and effective manner. As a result, the team is more effective because confusion, mistakes and indecision is minimised.

An important aspect in planning is how much of this function to share with team members. A plan may begin with you having developed it and announcing it and then over time move to a situation where team members manage the plan.

Accountability

Everything has to be accountable. Removing slop from a plan keeps it running efficiently and maximises effort in terms of productivity. You should always maintain influence in order to ensure accountability, but balanced against allowing the team to take some ownership and responsibility for the plan's delivery.

The Main Effort

I always invest considerable time in the planning stages. I make time for regular meetings to discuss how the plan is developing, identify any areas that need further analysis and agree the allocation of resources. I find it useful to brief my teams on what the 'main effort' is at that particular time. This helps focus efforts and make best use of the resources available for a task.

Knowledge and Information Sharing

Another important skill is to create an environment in which team members can share knowledge and information. An environment in which team members have situational awareness of each other's roles and appreciation for what they bring to the team promotes team synergy.

This considerably increases individual performance and maximises collective team performance and outputs. Cross training often ensures that in times of absences gaps are covered. However, I would suggest you implement situational awareness through wider techniques.

When I am working with geographically dispersed teams, where face-to-face meetings are not frequent, I ask team members or project leaders to provide regular updates on their tasks, both achievements and setbacks. Sharing achievements across the team provides encouragement, and sharing setbacks allows other members to contribute in finding a solution.

This knowledge sharing helps to develop team cohesion, generate motivation and build individual and collective confidence.

Planning

Learn from others
Draw on the experiences and skills within the team to put the plan together.

Forward plan
Answer the 'what, why, where, who, when and how' to provide a road map to goals.

Resource appropriately
Ensure that the team has the right resources for them to succeed in the task. This includes training, equipment, support and time.

Do not forget the detail
Spend time to focus on the small details.

Have a reserve
Always have a reserve to compensate for setbacks when they occur.

Summary
Understand the outcome

- Start out with the end in mind.
- Organisation is the best way to understand the outcome.
- Time spent on research is seldom wasted.
- If you fail to plan, you are planning to fail.
- Make everything accountable.
- Create an environment of knowledge and information sharing.
- For effective planning, learn from others, forward plan, resource, do not forget the small details and always have a reserve.

Notes

Chapter 13

Respect Individual Differences

"It is common to bring in team members with similar characteristics, as they are easier to work with. But you do need alternative perspectives to move forward productively."

Many of us grew up believing in the maxim taught at our mother's knee, treat people the way 'you' like to be treated. Yet this rule assumes that everybody wants to be treated the same way you do. Far more relevant is the concept that we should treat people the way 'they' would like to be treated.

Whether they are people from different cultures, or simply someone with a different viewpoint, listen to what they have to say. Very few, if any, people go to work, intent on screwing up. Equally, is there such a thing as a bad idea? I would suggest not. Likewise, an idea may be inappropriate, may need some further work, and so on, but people do not deliberately come up with bad ideas.

Team Engagement

Working as a team is not about liking people. It helps, but it is not necessary. However, what are necessary are engaged team members who recognise that everyone has a contribution to make. Individual and team engagement gains long-term commitment. An engaged team will perform better, be more positive, be less likely to fail and will deliver high performance consistently.

Team members will be proud to be part of the team; they will promote the fact to others and always go that extra mile to ensure success. Individual commitment levels will be higher because they will be more determined to remain part of the successful team and not replaced by others. Embracing the value of diversity and individual and team engagement will see tangible results very quickly.

Push and Pull

Skiing to the South Pole requires you to 'pull' all the equipment and supplies for the journey behind you in a sledge.

On the journey, you must continually alter course to find the easiest path through the crevasse fields, sastrugi or ice rubble. Sometimes the sledge moves effortlessly behind and other times more effort is required to pull it forward over an obstacle.

Sometimes it even requires a 'push' to overcome larger obstacles if there is no other easy course or if resources are limited and you cannot afford to take the easier route.

If you are to reach the Pole before food and fuel supplies run out you must maintain forward momentum.

The same applies to leadership. You 'pull' teams as you lead, setting direction and looking forward in an effort to avoid the obstacles that lay ahead. However, there will also be occasions when the environment, resources or deadlines requires you to 'push' in order to maintain forward momentum. To become effective at pushing or pulling you must have a good understanding and awareness of team members.

Only by first understanding the behaviours of team members, can you develop the right behaviours so that individuals and teams perform to their full potential.

Margerison-McCann

A number of psychometric models and tools are available on the market that can aid the leader in understanding behaviours.

One that I regularly use is the *Margerison-McCann Team Management Profile* that takes into account teamwork functions necessary to achieve results on a task. The model identifies eight factors based on broad teamwork functions and these eight factors form the *Types of Work Wheel*.

In identifying these eight factors and team functions, the model suggests the need to match work functions to individual abilities. At the centre of the wheel is a ninth factor called 'linking'. The Linker's function requires integrating the team effort. Other popular models are:

Myer Briggs Type Indicator (MBTI)

MBTI is helpful for individuals and teams needing to adapt quickly to new and changing environments. It gives knowledge on individual personality preferences, which when applied to team contexts shows diversity and performance potential for teams.

Strength Deployment Inventory (SDI)

SDI helps identify personal strengths in relating to others and when everything is going well, and when individuals are faced with conflict. It also suggests ways that one can deploy personal strengths to greatest effect and improve relationships with others.

Using profiles

> ### Share profiles
> Give each team member an A4 photo sheet, with contact details and profile role to prompt effective communication.

> ### Compensate for missing roles
> Profiling tools are useful project planning tools. Consider adding an agenda item in your meetings to ensure that you cover any role gaps.

> ### Create 'likes and dislikes'
> Create a profile for each team member, listing their likes and dislikes as a useful mental reminder to improve communications.

> ### Use profiles every day
> Highlight the importance of good communications by having a constant visual reminder of the profile logo.

Summary
Respect individual differences

- Treat people the way they would like to be treated.
- Few people go to work intent on screwing up.
- Engagement delivers long-term commitment.
- To achieve tangible results embrace the value of diversity and engagement.
- Understanding team members enables you to push or pull.
- To develop the right behaviours first understand the existing behaviours.
- Share profiles, compensate for missing roles, create 'likes and dislikes' notes and use profiles daily.

Notes

Chapter 14

Enjoy the Experience

"People are people and the key to getting them to perform at higher levels is the same whether they're skiing across the Arctic or working in an office."

Whatever else you may take away from this book, never forget the final 'E' of the mnemonic. If a leader is not enjoying what they are doing, the chances are that they are not doing a very good job. They may be giving it their best shot, but how much more effective would their business be if their employees enjoyed their work and felt proud to work for them?

Real breakthroughs come from leaders who enjoy doing what they do best, so make sure you put the effort in to putting round pegs in round holes.

A Sense of Humour

A sense of humour allows you to come to terms with demanding situations. Team members notice and it helps avoid setbacks spiralling out of control into much bigger problems.

Everyone has his or her own particular sense of humour. This is not about becoming the team comedian; it is more a case of not being serious all the time.

Story Telling

Another useful way to sustain values within a team is by telling stories, and having one for every occasion. A good one is the one that reflects an understanding of you. Stories about experiences can also be used to great effect during the early development of a team. Stories are a crucial means to communicate knowledge, skills, and most importantly the attributes so necessary to achieving high performance.

Motivation

The ability to motivate is what transforms a leader into the high performance leader. Motivation, of course, is a highly complex area and the subject of a book in its own right. I need to add a few words about it here because it is such an essential element of being a leader.

Motivation comes from within but a leader plays a significant role in influencing motivation in individuals. Everyone is motivated, and de-motivated, by different factors. What works for one person may not work for another.

To motivate is to pump people up. It aims people towards a goal and then fires them toward it like a rifle shot. Too often, the people listening do not share the courage of the leader who is doing the pumping and aiming. When the pump is away, the people deflate. More people need lifting up than pumping up. This is what inspiration does.

The challenge is to identify what motivates team members and take steps to provide that factor. However, individual motivators change through their life and as external influences are applied. It is a useful practice to seek feedback from team members regularly on what motivates or de-motivates them.

Capturing Why

When forming a new team, I ask everyone to write on a piece of paper, in private, what 'motivated' them to join the adventure and to refer to it regularly. Maybe it is a personal ambition to achieve a remarkable journey, to prove to themselves that they can, or just seeking fame.

The reason is not what matters, what is important is that they identify the spark that motivated them to take action in the first place. By carrying this reminder with them and referring to it, particularly when times are tough, will help keep the spark alive and provide inner motivation to keep moving forwards towards success.

Hauling a heavily laden sledge for 12 hours each day in blizzard conditions can be quite an isolating experience and it is equally important to have time for some light-hearted fun to take your mind off the challenges ahead.

At the end of each day, once all the chores are completed, we listen to music, share stories and take time to enjoy the experience and each other's company.

Motivation

✓ **Be motivated yourself**

A motivated leader will transcend to the team and encourage them to achieve higher levels of performance.

✓ **Select motivated people**

A team of motivated individuals will achieve higher levels of performance

✓ **Set challenging goals**

Generally, people want to achieve what is expected. Challenging goals will encourage your team to work hard to accomplish them.

✓ **Recognise progress**

Sharing success collectively enhances team cohesion and inspiration for forward momentum.

✓ **Give recognition**

Catch team members doing something right and tell them.

Summary
Enjoy the experience

- A sense of humour allows you to come to terms with demanding situations.
- Stories about experiences can help develop and sustain teams.
- Everyone is motivated, and de-motivated, by different factors.
- Identify what motivates others and provide that factor.
- Seek feedback from team members on what motivates or de-motivates them.
- Be motivated, select motivated people, set challenging goals, recognise progress and give recognition.

Notes

Chapter 15

Goals & Milestones

"Setting goals that are within immediate reach is critical to creating a high performance team."

Goal setting is another great technique in the leader's toolbox. Goals are essentially the steps required to achieve your vision. Goals can consist of two types; 'have to' goals and 'want to' goals and there is a critical difference between them.

Goals set by the team ('want to' goals) rather than goals imposed by others ('have to' goals) are the most effective. They relate to things a team wants to achieve rather than those you have to.

Milestones

In order to reach a goal it is useful to use milestones. In essence, milestones take a team closer towards achieving its goal; in other words, they are stepping-stones. Sometimes milestones must be executed in a set order to move in a determined direction, and at other times, there will be a choice.

Different ways of achieving the milestones are also likely to demand the completion of a different list of tasks before achieving success.

Milestones are either specified or implied. Specified milestones set out the order in which to achieve a task. Implied milestones enable the completion of specified milestones. Generally, you need only to be aware of implied milestones. A logical check of the task should reveal the implied milestones.

One Step to the Pole

When setting out on ultra long distance ski journeys I break the route down into specific milestones, usually landmarks or degrees of latitude. As we pass each milestone I make a real issue of celebrating the occasion.

Although hauling all your supplies on a long polar journey does mean you have to limit what you can take I always take along a selection of small luxuries such as a small cake, fresh coffee or cheese for such occasions.

Initially when we sit around the map each evening in our tent discussing the following day's activities I only show a small section of what lays ahead – the section leading up to the next milestone. To show the entire route of a 1,000 mile journey can be quite daunting to face.

As the journey unfolds I make a point of showing the entire map of what ground we have covered as a visual reminder to my teams of what milestones we have achieved so far. This helps build a positive attitude and desire to keep moving forwards. All of my adventures consist of individuals who have not completed such an undertaking before, but through using milestones and goals I know that polar success can be achieved by almost anyone.

SMART goals

Specific

The clearer the goal is visualised the greater will be the motivation to achieve it.

Measurable

To achieve a goal, a certain amount to a certain standard, is required to provide precise qualitative criteria.

Achievable

Beware of setting an impossible goal; make sure the goal is close enough to be attainable.

Realistic

Having assessed the 'achievability' of the goal, examine other commitments – such as timeframes.

Time-based

Set a stretching deadline otherwise, there will be no sense of urgency.

Summary
Goals and
milestones

- Goals consist of two types, 'have to' goals and 'want to' goals.
- Goals relating to things you want to achieve, rather than those you have to achieve, are more effective.
- Milestones are what take you closer towards a goal.
- Specified milestones set out the order in which to achieve a task.
- Implied milestones enable the completion of specified milestones.
- SMART goals are specific, measurable, achievable, realistic and time-based.

Notes

Chapter 16

Tent-time

"The most important question I ask my team is how we can we improve."

Having set milestones it is necessary to ensure that they are completed. It is not always effective to wait until the end of a task to evaluate. A review approach I have adopted on expeditions, for which I have coined the phrase *tent-time*, is a way to manage progress towards the completion of the task.

Using tent-time, can improve the completion of tasks when working towards achieving milestone. It enables a leader, and a team, to learn from mistakes and ensure they are not repeated in future tasks. In simple terms, tent-time is 'time out' to review feasibility and performance, listen to feedback, recognise success, learn from failure and modify plans accordingly.

It is important that planning allows for tent-time to take place and in the most objective manner possible.

Feedback

Feedback on performance is the basis on which team members understand how they are performing and what areas they need to improve on, and what is going on within the team and how they are contributing to wider team goals and objectives. Seeking feedback from a wide net will enable a leader and team members to learn lessons and avoid the repetition of mistakes.

Tent-time provides evidence to justify a pathway to success with potential setbacks and difficulties readily highlighted. Individual awareness and mutual understanding increases and communications improve.

Monitoring and recognising progress reinforces team cohesion and builds confidence. If an individual, or an entire team, is failing to meet set milestones it is necessary to find out why, and then perhaps set new milestones

Firstly, it needs to be ascertained that individuals understand objectives and secondly that they are aware of the gap between performance and objectives.

Explore with your team ways in which any gap can be closed and ensure any external factors influencing performance are explored and dealt with.

Also, evaluate factors that affect the tasks. In a business scenario, the factors may include the competition, the customer, budgets, the availability of resources and time. This process should lead to deductions of further tasks and constraints.

Pathways

By evaluating these factors, teams can find several pathways for achieving success as well as those that cannot achieve success. Pathways to success are possible solutions. A leader may have several pathways open, each of which would fulfil the task. The selection of the best pathway helps a leader and a team to develop a plan.

Discount and ignore pathways that will not work and focus efforts on those that will. To select the best pathways, compare and contrast the advantages and disadvantages of each one.

Steps to improvement

1. Reflect on progress made

Briefly review progress to share achievements and identify progress against agreed milestones.

2. Review future milestones

Reassess the plan to towards the next milestone is still valid and achievable.

3. Share feedback

Encourage open and honest feedback throughout the team.

4. Look for improvement

Always look for ways in which to improve progress towards goals.

Summary
Tent-time

- Tent-time is 'time out' to review progress and modify plans accordingly.
- Tent-time manages progress towards goals.
- To avoid repeating mistakes learn from them during tent-time.
- Feedback on performance is the basis of success.
- There are always several pathways to achieving success.
- Effective tent-time is about reflecting on progress, reviewing future milestones, sharing feedback and continually looking for areas to improve on.

Notes

Chapter 17

Team Cohesion

"If the people on your team share the same goals,
passion and desire to win you are
going to succeed."

The success of high performance teams ultimately depends on how well individuals of the team work together. This togetherness, or cohesion, is what binds individuals into a team and provides resilience against setbacks and obstacles. Many of the techniques and insights that I have shared in this book, such as the team charter and leadershift, contribute to developing and sustaining team cohesion.

However, understanding how to employ techniques is equally important. Success at creating team cohesion will be in knowing what techniques to use, when to use them and how to bring them all together.

Team cohesion will not happen overnight. It takes time. It takes effort. It requires you to remain alert to the unseen within the team, the hidden tensions, the unspoken words and interpersonal relationships. By having a feeling for the dynamic of a team, and applying the appropriate techniques to influence team cohesion, teams can be inspired to achieve remarkable achievements.

Having informal gatherings help to reinforce team cohesion. If people communicate with each other informally, they will work with each other positively when difficulties arrive.

Building team cohesion

❖ **Have a common purpose**

A common purpose will unite a team. People tend to create their own without one and cohesion breaks down.

❖ **Share success**

Share success to develop team confidence and share setbacks to develop determination and the commitment to succeed.

❖ **Build friendships**

Build friendships and collective bonding to encourage team members to work together and create a sense of belonging and ownership.

Summary
Team cohesion

- The success of teams ultimately depends on how well individuals of the team work together.
- Creating team cohesion is about knowing what techniques to use, when to use them and how to bring them all together.
- Remain alert to the dynamics within the team.
- Informal gatherings help to reinforce team cohesion.
- Building team cohesion requires a common purpose, share success and build friendships.

Notes

Chapter 18

Conclusion

"I am always looking at how I can develop myself to be a better leader and a better person."

As we have seen, leadership is a multi-faceted, learned skill that needs continual training, development and upkeep. You do not become a leader one day and then you are done.

The great thing about being a leader is that it is not the reserve of a select country club. Anyone can be a leader but, in my experience, you need to master the skills and insights set out in this book to be an effective one. These are the bread and butter of leadership.

Without these, when the going gets tough, you will flounder. However, with them, as I have demonstrated repeatedly you can take your vision and your team to the peak of performance.

I hope that the insights that I have shared in this masterclass support your journey in creating, developing, sustaining and leading high performance teams. Enjoy the journey and keep exploring.

Chapter 19

Resources

Maslow's Theory

There are many theories around positive motivation but Abraham Maslow created a series of consecutive fundamental needs that constitute the best known. In order to enable people to be happy in their work and in personal life there are five sets of basic human needs. These are fundamental in the sense that they are needs that everyone possesses, or which are at least potentially present in everyone.

All the needs link dynamically. They supersede each other in a fixed order; a 'higher' need only comes to the fore once a 'lower' need has become satisfied. When a need has been satisfied, it no longer constitutes a motivating factor. Someone who is hungry will put effort into finding food. Once fed, he will no longer possess the motivation to search for food. However this should not see this 'dominating' of lower needs over 'higher' needs as something absolute but rather as relative.

The consecutive nature of need requirement is something that can be followed in the development of an individual from baby to adult. The higher up the hierarchy, the more important the need, to the extent that a lower need can be sacrificed for a high need.

Physiological

This is food, drink, warmth, rest and shelter, i.e. things that have to be satisfied at a basic level of function.

Safety and Security

This is a need for stability in life. A need to understand order and the inherent freedoms and constraints that these place on an individual.

Social

If the previous two stages are met then the individual realises the need to belong and to be loved within the framework of a family/work setting, therefore does not feel lonely or outcast.

Esteem

This is a basic desire not to feel helpless or inferior and a desire to want responsibility and self-elevation. The desire for competence and achievement of personal independence and freedom, and the desire for respect from others.

Self-realisation (self-actualisation)

This is simply the need for an individual to realise his full potential and the desire for self-fulfilment

Leadership styles

Democratic

Democratic leaders make the final decision after inviting members to contribute to the decision-making process.

Bureaucratic

Bureaucratic leaders work by the book, ensuring teams follow procedures. The inflexibility can demoralise teams and their ability to react to changes.

Autocratic

This is where a leader exerts high levels of power with individuals in the team giving few opportunities for making suggestions.

Laissez-faire

This French phrase means 'leave it be' and describes the leader who leaves the team to get on with their work. It can be effective providing monitoring and communications are regular.

Servant

This term is used to describe someone who leads by meeting the needs of the team. It is a form of democratic leadership, as the whole team tends to be involved in decision-making.

People oriented

This style of leadership has the leader either totally focused on organising and developing the people in the team or focusing only on getting the job done.

Charismatic

A charismatic leader injects enthusiasm into the team, and is very energetic in driving others forward. Charismatic leaders can believe more in themselves than in their team.

Leadership attributes

Innovation

This is about being creative in how you manage situations, lead change, take risks and encourage others to take risks.

Decision Making

This is an ability to handle complexity, uncertainty and ambiguity. When evaluating information showing clarity of thought, decisiveness and judgement.

Vision

This is about creating a shared picture of success using it to clarify boundaries for self and others.

Humility

This is about not being arrogant or condescending to others, but treating others with respect and appreciating other contributions.

Integrity

Integrity is about moral courage, appropriate values and standards to inspire and reciprocate loyalty.

Develop focus

A leader focused on individual and team development can create a culture and climate that enables people to develop their potential.

Professional knowledge

This attribute is the wisdom to correctly apply knowledge and experience in any current context and understand the full implications of actions.

Communication

This is about negotiation, influencing and persuading, networking and mentoring. It is also about active listening, encouraging idea generation and feedback.

Explore more on Sean

www.seanchapple.co.uk

Sean's talks, workshops and adventures are inspirational and offer powerful learning so you can explore the business of winning teams for yourself.

Insights

Whether you are preparing and executing a business strategy, managing a new project, or putting together a team to make a record-breaking attempt on the South Pole, you can benefit from Sean's lifetime of team building at the edge. Share lessons on leading for high-performance in Sean's online resources library.

Speaking

Through motivational speaking, Sean shares the secrets of overcoming setbacks to achieve success against the odds. His keynotes offer inspirational and powerful learning in self-motivation, risk-assessment, team building and leadership. Against the inspirational backdrop of his record-breaking polar journeys, Sean outlines practical insights for unleashing the full potential in individuals and teams.

Development

Polar adventure is about getting results from limited resources, motivating teams to higher levels of performance, and maintaining optimism in fast-changing environments. Sean leads and supports multi-day experiential leadership and team development interventions where business audiences can learn from his lifetime of extreme achievement.

Adventures

Sean's expeditions involve real leadership and team development in the world's most unforgiving environments. Through calculated risk-taking, Sean and the expedition team will extend your boundaries of endurance, self-confidence, learning and initiative and lead you on a life-changing journey. Join Sean on a journey beyond the horizon. Destinations include the North Pole, South Pole, Iceland, Greenland and Siberia.

To explore more visit www.seanchapple.co.uk

Feedback from Others

'Arresting but beguiling; without leaving the room, Sean effortlessly takes audiences on some of the perilous journeys he has taken, giving them an at-times painfully honest account of his treks across frozen lands.'
England

'Sean's content was a great fit to our development programme. His workshop was inspiring, entertaining and included a wealth of lessons on the challenges of high performance team working.'
Portugal

'Sean did the keynote at our conference for professional consultants from Germany, Austria and Switzerland. Everyone agreed - the speech was the highlight of the day, with lots of meaningful insights...and fun!
Germany

'Sean is a regular guest speaker at the London Business School. His inspirational talk offers a fascinating perspective on the challenges of leadership which offers real value to our senior executives and managers attending one of our programmes.'
England

'Using Sean as a motivational speaker at our sales conference provided the perfect example to demonstrate that through applying self drive, planning and teamwork you can succeed. The personal account of his experience and the approach he took to meeting his goal enabled the audience to identify with their own personal challenges and feel motivated to being able to achieve them.'

Belgium

'Sean brought a new dimension in leadership to our Management Conference. Not only did he give a fascinating description of his polar expedition, he was able to relate how leadership in such extreme circumstances applies to more 'normal' business situations...I have no hesitation in highly recommending Sean to their organisations.'

England

'Visiting Florida, I was able to get the 'Ice Man' to really warm up a local audience. His insight into leadership and teamwork based on his polar adventures created a sense of awe in the group. Sean's wit and engaging personality kept the audience excited and energized. Thanks for the instant energy!'

United States of America

My fellow adventurers

Unfortunately, there is not enough space to mention all those who have joined me over the years on my journey to becoming a business adventurer. I hope that in this final chapter of *Leading High Performance Teams* I can adequately thank my fellow business adventurers who have accompanied and supported me on some remarkable journeys.

1st/2nd Parkeston Scout Group
Donald Palmer, Barney, Brian Mayo.

Grand Canyon Challenge Expedition
Sir Jimmy Saville OBE, Chris Ray, Robert Forward, Andy Fletcher, Roy Osborne.

Karakoram Expedition
Paul Mattin, Neil MacMillan, Neil Peacock.

Northern Trails Expedition
Dace Thomas, Tim Welford, Alan Chambers, Rayson Pritchard, John Claire.

Icelandic 500 Expedition
Diana Princess of Wales, Sir Jimmy Saville OBE, Michael Aspel, Lieutenant General Sir Robert Ross KCB OBE, Nick Arding OBE, Dave Thomas, Tim Welford, Alan Chambers, Steve Jones, Ian

Robinson, Alan Thomson, Craig Payne, Mark, Stuckey, Steve Crouden, Rory Bruce, John Blashford-Snell MBE, Dr Mike Stroud, Roger Mear, Roger Daynes, Ingi Thor Thorgrimsson, Jon Gunnar Egilsson, Mike O'Reilly, Thrustor Reynisson.

Frozen Fields Expedition

Andy Pillar OBE, Nick Arding OBE, Aziz 'Ozzie' Kheraj, Terry Jesudason, Alan Chambers, Jason Garland, Dave Davenport, Tony Lang, Dave Trevellion, Alan Keir, Pete Carr, Keith Ewart, Pete Norman, Andy Noyes, Peter Morris, Roger Daynes, Morag Howell.

Polar Communicate Expedition

Alan Chambers, Jason Garland, Dave Davenport, Tony Lang, Dave Trevellion, Russ Freeth, Alan Keir, Pete Carr, Keith Ewart, Pete Norman, Peter Morris, Morag Howell, Flo Howell.

Polar North Expedition

HRH Prince Phillip, Major General David Pennefather CB OBE, Nick Arding OBE, Terry Jesudason, Alan Chambers, Jason Garland, Dave Davenport, Tony Lang, Dave Trevellion, Alan Keir, Dr Howard Oakley, Pete Carr, Keith Ewart, Pete Norman, Andy Noyes, David Wilson, Clive Gill, Roger Daynes, Morag Howell, Flo Howell.

Polarwatch Expedition

Sir Ranulph Fiennes, Colonel John Blashford-Snell OBE, Nick Arding OBE, Dave Davenport, Pete Carr, Keith Ewart, Terry Jesudason, Ann Diver, Kevin Hayter, Mark Cotton, Gina English, Will Rigby, John Rigby, Guy Beeching, Abigail Davey, Claire

Wilson, Fran Johnson.

Polar Quest North Expedition
Admiral Sir James Burnell-Nugent CBE, Lieutenant General Gary Robison ADC, Nick Arding OBE, Barrie Whitehead, David Poke, Jim Bonney, Aziz "Ozzie" Kheraj, Rob McIntyre, Ben McDonald, John Carroll, Matthew Vivian, Phil Towers, Ed Reed, Richard Howard, Jock Easton, Mark Freeman, Nathan Simms, Greg Fenton, Jerry Heal, Chris Cook.

Polar Watch Expedition
Tony Alexander, Andrew Davies, Paul Jeffery, Joan England, Sarah Rogers, Aziz 'Ozzie' Kheraj, Ady Cole MBE, Liane Dry, Tara Woodard, Sarah Beresford, Harry Gates, James Kelly, Andy Gardner, Matthew Kain, Kizzie Peters, Lucy O'Callaghan, Katrina Taylor, Alistair Douglas, Allan McClelland, Simon Lewis, David Tucker, Carly Whittle, Ben Davis, Sarah Withers, Tim Chapman, Tom Rock, Rachael Murrin, Judith Lancaster, Harry Gates, Penny Hill, Steve Ford, Vicki Peabody, Sarah Beresford, Sam Heasman.

Polar Quest South Expedition
The Princess Royal, Admiral Sir James Burnell-Nugent CBE, Lieutenant General Gary Robison ADC, Nick Arding OBE, Pete Roberts, Andy Brown, Craig Hunter, Paul Mattin, Greg Fenton, Jerry Heal, Suzie Thomson, Polly Hatchard, Ross Kane, Jock Easton, Mark Freeman, Niklas Norman, Neil Godbold, Dave Pearce, Bear Grylls, Sue Stockdale, Ben Saunders, Mike Sharp.

Major sponsors of my journeys

TMS Development International, Stræker, British Petroleum, Falklands Oil & Gas Company, WL Gore, Royal Navy & Royal Marines, Sir Donald Gosling, Bernard Sunley Foundation, Beacons Products Limited, Biltong, Brands Home & Leisure Ltd, Brenig, Eurotech, Hardigg Storm Cases, Fra Angelico Limited, Harcoster Drums Limited, Lowe Alpine Group (UK) Ltd, NSSL, Paracademy, Sodexho Defence,

My mentors

Nick Arding OBE, Bronco Lane MM BEM, Conrad Dickinson, Keith Ewart, Dave Davenport, Frank Furness, Cathy O'Dowd.

Charities supported on Sean's journeys

Childhood Cancer Research, International Spinal Research Trust, The White Ensign Association, The UK Antarctic Heritage Trust.

Further reading

Polar Quest – Journey to the Poles

ISBN : 978-1-4092-2448-8

Polar Quest chronicles Sean's groundbreaking adventures to the magnetic North Pole and the geographical South Pole in the same year - the South Pole journey is one of the longest overland journeys in polar history. This a fascinating account based on live reports sent during the journey and personal diary extracts.

No Ordinary Tourist

ISBN : 978-1-4092-2453-2

Thought to be an impossible journey Sean completed one of the last remaining great ski adventures – an epic ski across Iceland from west to east coasts. For 47 days Sean lead his team through blizzards, hail storms and rain as they crossed mountain ranges, glaciers and the harsh Icelandic interior. Candid extracts from Sean's daily personal journal provide a unique insight into the entire amazing journey, its near disasters, and its ultimate success.